A+ Alphabet Books

Toys ABC

An Alphabet Book

by B. A. Hoena

Consulting Editor: Gail Saunders-Smith, PhD

Capstone press

Mankato, Minnesota

A is for
action figures.

Grab your action figures. Bend their elbows
and straighten their knees. They're ready
for action. Are you ready to play?

B is for bicycle.

Hop on your bicycle and go for a ride.
Say hello to friends as you pedal by.

C is for car.

Cars zip around the track, trying to win the race. They could crash if they go too fast. **ZOOM!**

D is for doll.

This doll is ready for the day. Her hair is braided, and she's dressed to play.

E is for easel.

An easel holds paper while you paint.
Then you can create a work of art.

F is for finger paints.

Dip your fingers into finger paints.
You can make colorful pictures,
smearing paint across the paper.

G is for glove.

Look up! It's a high fly ball.
Get back! Use your glove
to catch the ball.

H is for hoop.

The basketball sails toward the hoop.
If it goes through, you score. **SWISH!**

I is for in-line skates.

Strap on your in-line skates.
Now you have wheels
on your feet. You roll
wherever you want to go.

J is for jigsaw puzzle.

Ask a friend to help you with a jigsaw puzzle.
Snap the pieces together to see the picture.

K is for kite.

A gust of wind lifts your kite
into the air. Let out some string,
so it can fly higher and higher.

L is for logs.

Use logs to build. You can make
a fort or a home for tiny toy people.

M is for microphone.

Sing into a microphone and pretend you're a star. It makes your voice loud, so everyone can hear.

N is for neon glow stick.

Neon glow sticks are out of sight!
Twirl them around to light up the night.

O is for octopus.

A stuffed octopus has eight fuzzy arms for you to hold. What's your favorite stuffed toy?

P is for pogo stick.

Jump on a pogo stick to bounce off the ground. Count how many times you bounce up and down. One. Two. Three....

Q is for queen.

In the game of chess, the queen is a powerful piece. It moves forward or backward, sideways or diagonally.

R is for rocket.

The rocket is ready to launch.
It's time to begin the countdown.
Five. Four. Three. Two. One.
BLAST OFF!

S is for
skateboard.

Get on your skateboard and go for a ride.
Show friends the tricks you can do.

T is for train.

A train engine chugs around the tracks.
It's pulling boxcars and a caboose.
CHOO CHOO!

U is for ukulele.

Is it a tiny guitar? No, it's a ukulele.
This instrument is often used to play
Hawaiian music.

V is for video game.

You can do fun things in a video game. Blast away space aliens or play your favorite football team.

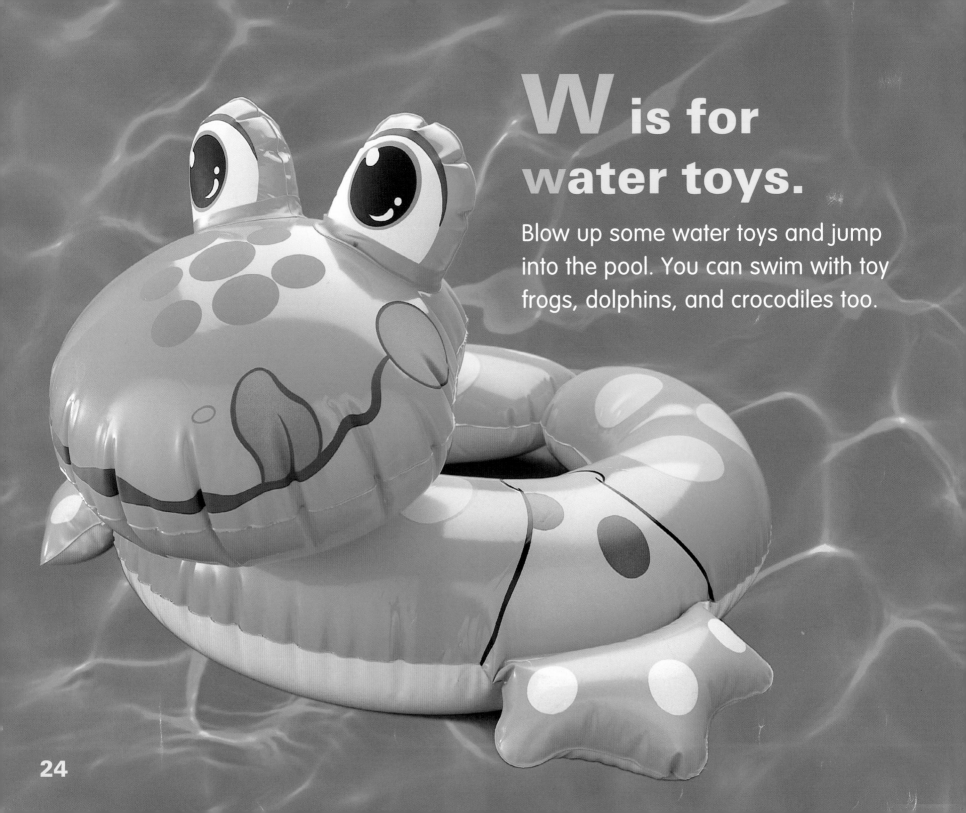

W is for water toys.

Blow up some water toys and jump into the pool. You can swim with toy frogs, dolphins, and crocodiles too.

X is for X.

Mark an X in an empty square
to start a game of tic-tac-toe.
You win if you get three in a row.

25

Y is for yo-yo.

A yo-yo comes back to you when you toss it down. Hold on to the string and watch the yo-yo spin around.

Z **is for zoo.**

You can make your own toy zoo.
Gather some animals and invite
your friends to play with you.

Fun Facts about Toys

People believe that yo-yos are one of the world's oldest toys. The first yo-yos were made in China thousands of years ago. Stone yo-yos that are more than 2,000 years old have been found in Greece. In the 1500s, yo-yos were a popular toy for children in the Philippines. "Yo-yo" actually means "come come" in Filipino. Yo-yos were first brought to the United States in the 1920s.

The first jigsaw puzzles were made by mapmakers in the mid-1700s. They pasted maps onto wood boards. The pieces of the puzzle were then cut one at a time by hand. Children learned about geography from early jigsaw puzzles.

In the late 1800s, bicycles had iron frames and wood wheels. These bicycles were so rough to ride that people called them "boneshakers."

Some stories say that ukulele means "jumping flea." When Hawaiians first saw this instrument played, they noticed how the fingers of the musician moved very fast. They thought the person's fingers were jumping around like fleas, so they named the instrument "ukulele."

Scott and Brennan Olson made the first in-line skates. These brothers were from Minnesota and played hockey. They made in-line skates similar to ice skates so they could work on their ice-skating skills during the summer.

The world's biggest kite is large enough to hold a small jet airplane.

Glossary

boxcar (BOKS-car)—a train car with a sliding door on one side; boxcars are used to carry goods.

caboose (kuh-BOOSS)—the last car on a train

chess (CHESS)—a game for two people with 16 pieces each and played on a board; each player has one queen.

diagonal (dye-AG-uh-nuhl)—a line that joins opposite corners of a square or rectangle

easel (EE-zuhl)—a folding stand used to hold a painting

engine (EN-juhn)—the front part of a train that pulls the cars

gust (GUHST)—a strong blast of wind

microphone (MYE-kruh-fone)—an instrument used to make sounds louder, such as a person's voice

Read More

Doney, Meryl. *Toys.* Crafts from Many Cultures. Milwaukee: Gareth Stevens, 2004.

Nelson, Robin. *Toys and Games Then and Now.* First Step Nonfiction. Minneapolis: Lerner, 2003.

Steele, Philip. *Toys and Games.* Everyday History. New York: F. Watts, 1999.

Internet Sites

FactHound offers a safe, fun way to find Internet sites related to this book. All of the sites on FactHound have been researched by our staff.

Here's how:
1. Visit *www.facthound.com*
2. Type in this special code **0736826092** for age-appropriate sites. Or enter a search word related to this book for a more general search.
3. Click on the **Fetch It** button.

FactHound will fetch the best sites for you!

Index

A+ Books are published by Capstone Press
151 Good Counsel Drive, P.O. Box 669, Mankato, Minnesota 56002
www.capstonepub.com

Library of Congress Cataloging-in-Publication Data
Hoena, B. A.
  Toys ABC: an alphabet book / by B.A. Hoena.
  p. cm.—(A+ alphabet books)
  Includes bibliographical references and index.
  ISBN-13: 978-0-7368-2609-9 (hardcover)
  ISBN-10: 0-7368-2609-2 (hardcover)
  1. Toys—Juvenile literature. 2. Alphabet books—Juvenile literature. [1. Toys. 2. Alphabet.]
I. Title. II. Alphabet (Mankato, Minn.) III. Series.
GV1218.5.H64 2004
688.7'2—dc22   2003027801

Summary: Introduces toys through photographs and brief text that uses one word relating to toys
    for each letter of the alphabet.

Credits
Amanda Doering and June Preszler, editors; Heather Kindseth, designer; Kelly Garvin,
    photo researcher; Eric Kudalis, product planning editor

Photo Credits
Capstone Press/Gary Sundermeyer, cover, 1, 2, 4, 5, 6, 7, 8, 10, 11, 13, 14, 15, 16, 17, 18, 19, 20,
    21, 22, 23, 24, 25, 26, 28, 29
Corbis/Alan Schein Photography, 9
Photodisc Inc., 27
Rubberball, 3
Thinkstock, 12

Note to Parents, Teachers, and Librarians
Toys ABC: An Alphabet Book uses colorful photographs and a nonfiction format to
introduce children to characteristics about toys while building a mastery of the alphabet.
This book is designed to be read independently by an early reader or to be read aloud
to a pre-reader. The images help early readers and listeners understand the text and
concepts discussed. The book encourages further learning by including the following
sections: Fun Facts about Toys, Glossary, Read More, Internet Sites, and Index. Early
readers may need assistance using these features.